100 Love Sonnets
Pablo Neruda

Special thanks to Norm Minnick and Gus Brunsman for proofreading and editorial suggestions.
Also thanks to Robert Bly for introducing me to Neruda, and to Coleman Barks for his cosmic coffee shop visitations.

Designed and edited by Chris Jansen.

ISBN   978-1-300-55615-2

AFTERNOON

EVENING

NIGHT

phosphorus

INTRODUCTION

Find a Soulmate

There are many souls, both positive and negative, to whom we are inexplicably bound for life. Carl Jung describes the meeting of two persons like a chemistry experiment. The two personalities may be miscible or not; they may bubble and overflow; they may change color or become very hot or very cold; spread sweet smell like the singing, hand-holding ring of benzene, or the mixture simply may explode. When I first met Neruda there was an immediate reaction. I was introduced to him through Robert Bly's wonderful translations of *Odes to Common Things* (*Odas Elementales*), but because Bly's voice is so strong and distinctive this was more like meeting Bly than Neruda. It was as if Neruda stood quietly to the side and Bly spoke through one of his iconic masks, while Neruda silently nodded his assent. To meet the living Neruda I had to sit down and exchange words with him. I started fooling around with his poems (picking some at random, they turned out by chance or providence to be from *Cien Sonetos de Amor*) in their original Spanish and there was bubbling and a swirling band of color change from black to white to rose-red. As I added my soul in drop-wise, word by word, with Neruda's, there were tiny explosions and sweet smoke and I was left with something very heavy and substantial in my hands.

Reading published translations of the poems I was working on, I was surprised by how stilted they felt. Neruda's voice—his sea-deep, sea-vast voice, aching with humanity—felt as if it were crippled, shaking and falling while trying to stand up from a wheelchair. It's not that these translations are inaccurate, just that in in their weakened condition, hugging the safety rail of literality, they are unable to dance. I remembered the story of Robert Bly handing Coleman Barks a copy of an old translation of Rumi and giving him the charge: "these poems need to be freed from their cages." I learned quickly that a poem should not be awakened and dragged from its cage (this results in truly awful translations such as some

8

'modern' Bibles with their free associations and vulgar dumbed-down language). It's best if a poem is induced to come out of its cage with love and honesty and the promise of a good home.

Learn to Speak Lion

As I began to translate, I worked as if I had been asked to do a heart transplant on a beautiful young girl with only a set of books to guide me. I felt a tremendous burden of responsibility and I was terrified of making even one mistake; one tiny slip of mistranslation would be a dishonorable and dangerous contamination. When I came across a word or phrase for which there was no English equivalent, I went through a hand-wringing agon of translating, retranslating, cross-referencing with other translations, etymological research, and feeling around in the dark for scalpel, sponge and clamp. Eventually Jim Watt (English Professor emeritus at Butler University) overheard me expressing these concerns and supplied me with the following Neruda quote: "The true translation destroys the poem.". I felt something give way. It was as if Neruda had given me his blessing. "Look," I imagined him saying, "we both have the poet's disease. We are both lovers. You know what it is to be a lover, to have a woman made of words flowing through your crimson vessels. Now tell me my poems back to me." This is not to say that I continued with any less devotion to the accuracy of the translation, only that I felt I had Neruda's blessing to render some of his lines in my own American (southern American) idiom.

The philosopher Ludwig Wittgenstein said, "If a lion could speak we wouldn't understand him." Wittgenstein is suggesting that the consciousness of a lion—the concepts and ideas and emotions, lion-love lion-lust, lion-ache, lion-grief, the structure of lion-thought itself—would be untranslatable. This is true of poetry translations as well. Neruda and I are separated by time, by culture, by language, by the beauty and complexity of his soul. It's at this point I am expected to say that it is our commonalities that lay the foundation for my translation, but that would not be exactly true. I have taken Neruda's poems—living objects that they are—and metabolized them with my own body and produced a new and living creation. Neruda's hardships are in these poems, his political exile, his flight from Chile, his secret home in Santiago where he carried on his affair with Matilde ; the beach where the lovers walked is here; the salt spray and sea air suffuse these poems; each strophe is composed of timbers salvaged from the deep grave of shipwrecks. Neruda's ancestors are here too: his philandering father, his mother (a teacher who died two months after he was born, probably from an infection related to childbirth), his little girl, Malvina, born with severe deformities and who died at only eight years old, the wars that rolled across Europe killing many of his dearest friends and fellow poets, the treachery and betrayals of political life. But just as Coleman Barks's Rumi translations are informed by the music echoing from out of the Tennessee valleys where he was raised, there is the sound and feeling of my southwest Georgia childhood in my rendering of Neruda.

Quiet the world and listen closely to these poems: there is the uncanny music of the African-Americans I grew up with (itself freighted with a thousand years of nobility and sorrow); there is the vast, languid body of the Flint River a great green *pythos* full of catfish the size of small cattle, it writhes through the city center reviewing the graves of Civil War veterans and slaves as it passes; of blueholes, and kaolin springs, of Friday night high school football and limesinks (the city's foundation is a honeycomb of limestone— billions of micro-skeletons of billions of creatures that lived and fought and died billions of years ago) that occasionally is worn away by the secret rivers flowing underground—and a hole opens up and swallow a cow or a car; sweet scent of an opening magnolia and walking up on fat, languid cottonmouths; of swamps whose waters are so black they shine like mirrors in the afternoon sun, and alligators discovered in the swimming pool, and pecan orchards and a Baptist preacher-man preaching revival and blond Southern beauty queens, and again the maze of aquifer tunnels under the city where boys and men go exploring and their scuba tanks occasionally turn up but their bodies are never recovered. (*Almost* never recovered: a teenage life-guard named O. Victor Miller once braved a harrowing descent into the actual underworld to bring back an expolorer's body. Miller went on to become an English professor at Darton College, and one of my greatest teachers, friends and mentors.)

Thus I am a truth and Neruda is a truth and together we are something not seen before. You may like us or not, but these poems, unlike so many translations, are the music of our living souls—living and working and loving together.

If you can't be faithful at least be loving

Why are Southern women so enchanting? Matilde Urrutia, to whom these poems are addressed, was from Southern Chile, and this is one of her charms for Neruda. Southern women from any hemisphere are associated with beauty, mystery, wildness, strength and sensuality. Since Neruda was married at the time he began seeing Matilde, the couple was compelled to invent reasons to be in the same city at the same time. The secret nature of their affair added a layer of intensity and urgency to their relationship. From this intensity the Cien Sonetos de Amor were born (though Neruda delayed their publication in order to spare the feelings of his then wife).

It's worth noting that Neruda could be described as a womanizer prior to Matilde. Though not exactly endowed with movie star good looks, his passion and personal charm attracted women wherever he went. And having a poet's heart (and genitals), he felt obliged to be with as many admirers as possible. The really startling thing is that after two marriages and countless affairs he actually seemed to find the love he was looking for in Matilde. Matilde the singer, the guitarist, the cook, the gardener, the nurse: she often appears in these poems as a bridge between the living world of human beings and the living world of things.

Growing up in poverty, Neruda has an interesting relationship with the earth. He wants to love it, but as *Residence on Earth* shows, he is aware of the despair that underlies the natural world (see Virgil: "lacrima rerum"—the tears of things). Matilde is the one who justifies every hardship, who soothes every wound.

Neruda was haunted all his life by the horrors of the natural world. His mother died a few weeks after he was born, likely from puerperal or "child-bed" fever (you could say his birth caused her death). His student years are spent among a bunch of young consumptives, the invisible touch of any one of them possibly bringing death to the poet, whose health was never good. It's a miracle that he survived at all. And yet though he wrestles with nature, he does not make war on her. Women are the key to peace with the natural world. His step-mother makes his underwear out of empty grain sacks, and grain, with its resemblance to mycobacterium tuberculosis under the microscope, might easily stand for the malevolent fecundity of dumb nature. Instead it becomes a recurring image of love's abundance, the gravity of desire, the molecular weight of passion. But the queen of the natural world is Matilde. She is the emissary of God and nature. Other women had been intellectuals and activists, but with Matilde he must have felt like he was marrying the earth itself.

"Translation is like a woman. If it is beautiful, it is not faithful. If it is faithful, it is most certainly not beautiful." Most sources attribute this familiar quote to Russian poet Yevgeny Yevtushenko (a minority cite Moliere). Barks and Bly, working from literal, word-for-word translations address this axiom by calling their poems "versions" or "imitations". What I've learned from translating and studying translations is that every translation, including literal translation (*especially* literal translation) is a version. This doesn't justify simply incorrect or mistaken translation. There *are* wrong answers—though even in this I've seen (and made) lovely little fortunate mistakes. But these hybrids are new poems, variations on a theme, not proper translations, and it would be dishonest to call them anything else.

The only time I deliberately strayed from the original was in the case of idioms which simply could not be literally rendered. Neruda often uses the word racimos (translated: "bunches" or "bunches of grapes") to suggest a kind of ripe abundance. Unfortunately "bunches" simply doesn't translate elegantly in English. "I loved her intensely, now I have bunches." Hmmm. Perhaps you should see a doctor? I think you see the point—inappropriate laughter is the worst kind of response to a translation.

I keep invoking new metaphors here to describe this process and its product. Translation is a chemical reaction, a blood transfusion, a marriage, a love affair. This metaphor-making is how poets work. This is how you know we are in love. I'd like to suggest one last metaphor that among literature is unique to translations: a translation is like a 'cover' version of a song. By translating you harmonize and orchestrate. You sweeten, shade and color by singing the tune in your own voice. Singing this way is a real joy, an exercise in intimacy with the great man's soul. Musicians appreciate this miracle. The singer can't help but add his own unique mannerisms to the song. And some music feels as if it was made to be performed by other musicians. Rachmaninoff said, after hearing Vladimir Horowitz perform one of his concertos, that he himself could never play it again. And he didn't.

It's been my privilege to work with Neruda's songs of innocence and experience. I'd like these poems to persist, to affect the reader. I'd like them to land down deep in the reader's soul where they encode little moments of beauty for the future. I realize that's a lot to ask, and so if they fail to germinate and flower this way, I at least want them to provoke strong feelings, either for against the poems, for or against me, for or against my way of working. Even if these poems do none of these things, I pray that the reader will *find a soulmate, learn to speak lion, be loving,* and do his or her own translation of life into love, love into life.

13

Morning

1

Matilde, name of a plant or stone or wine,
of what is born from the earth, and lasts,
word in whose growth is dawn,
in which summer explodes from the light of lemons.

In the name of wooden ships
surrounded by swarms of blue fire
are letters, the waters of a river
that flows into my burned heart.

Oh name discovered under the ivy
like a door to the secret tunnel that communicates
with the fragrance of the world.

Oh invade me with your burning mouth,
search me, if you will, with your eyes of night,
only in your name let me sail and sleep.

2

Love, how many roads until you get to a kiss,
what loneliness wandering before your company.
Trains go on rolling alone with the rain.
In Taltal, no spring dawns.

But you and I, my love, we are together.
We are together from our clothes to our loins,
the together of autumn, of water, of hips,
until you are only you, and I am only I, together.

To think that it took all the rocks holding up the river,
the mouth of the Boroa,
to think that, separated by trains and nations,

you and I simply had to love,
along with all the confused men and women,
along with the earth that planted and raised its carnations.

3

Bitter love, violet crowned with thorns,
bushes bristling between so many passions,
shaft of pain, flower of rage,
how and in what ways do you direct my soul?

Why do you suddenly set your agonizing fires
between the cold leaves of my soul?
Who taught you the steps that led to me?
What flower, what stone, what smoke marked my home?

The truth is this: frightful night trembled
as the dawn filled our glasses with its wine
and the sun established its celestial presence,

while your cruel love surrounded me without mercy,
until I was cut with swords and spines
and a burning path was opened in my heart.

4

Remember that wild ravine
where the beating aroma climbed,
a sometimes-bird dressed
in water and slow winter clothes.

Remember the gifts of the earth:
irascible fragrance, gold clay,
grass of the thicket, wild roots,
gypsy spines like swords.

Remember the flowers you brought,
flowers of shadow and silent water,
a bouquet like a foam-covered rock.

That time was like never and always:
come with me, where we expect nothing
and find everything, there, waiting.

5

I did not touch the night, nor the air, nor the dawn,
only earth, apples that grow from hearing pure water,
the mud, the fragrant resins of your country.

From Fivepoints, where your eyes were formed,
To the Border, where your feet were created for me,
you are the dark clay that I know:
on your hips I touch all of the new harvest.

Maybe you did not know, little-puzzle-tree,
That even before I loved you, before I forgot your kisses,
my heart was remembering your mouth,

and went like a wounded man through the streets,
until I knew that I had found my love,
my country of kisses and volcanoes.

6

Lost in the woods, I cut off a dark branch
and lifted its soft whisper to my thirsty lips:
it was perhaps the voice of the rain crying,
a cracked bell, a torn heart.

It was something that had seemed so far away,
gravely hidden, covered by earth,
a cry muffled by immense autumns,
by the moist half-open darkness of the leaves.

Waking from the dreams of the forest,
that hazel branch sang under my mouth
and its fugitive smell climbed up for my enjoyment

as if suddenly I was sought out by the roots
abandoned in the lost ground of my childhood,
and I stopped, wounded by that wandering scent.

7

Come with me, I said. No one knew
where or how this pain was throbbing,
or how for me there were no carnations or love songs,
nothing but the wound that love had opened.

I repeated, Come with me, as if I was dying,
and nobody saw the bloody moon in my mouth,
or the blood filling up the silence.
Oh love, forget that thorny star!

At last, when I heard your voice repeating,
"Come with me"—it was as if you had unleashed
pain, love, the fury of sealed wine

that from its underground cellar rises,
and again in my mouth I felt the taste of fire,
of blood, of flowers, of stones and burning.

If it were not for your eyes the color of the moon,
and days of clay, of work, of fire;
if it were not that, though imprisoned, you have the agility of air
and a week's worth of amber,

if it wasn't for that yellow moment
in which the autumn vines rise
and you are the bread that the fragrant moon
makes as it moves along the flour of the sky,

oh my dearest, I would not love you so.
In your embrace I embrace all that exists,
sand, time, the tree of rain:

all things live so that I may live,
and without going so far as to see it all,
I see in your life every living thing.

9

At the breaking of a wave against the wild stone,
clarity bursts forth and establishes her rose,
and the circle of the sea is reduced to a few grapes,
a single blue drop of salt that has fallen.

Oh radiant magnolia unleashed in the foam,
beautiful traveler whose death blooms
and eternally returns, to be and to be nothing:
broken salt, dazzling sea movement.

My love, you and I together seal the silence
while the sea destroys its constant statues
and demolishes its towers of rage and calm,

because in the fabric of these invisible threads
there are lost waters and endless sands
in which we carry the sole persecuted tenderness.

10

Tender is the beautiful, as if music and wood,
agate, cloth, wheat, and transparent peaches
had erected a fugitive statue.
Against the wave she directs her contrary face.

The ocean polishes her tanned feet, their likeness
copied so soon in the sand,
and now she is the female fire of a rose,
a single bubble contending with the sun and sea.

Oh that nothing may touch you but the cold salt,
nor love destroy your pure spring.
Beautiful woman, echo of the endless foam,

let your hips arrange upon the sea
a new measure —of swan, of lily—
and drive this form through the endless waters.

11

I have hungered for your mouth, your voice, your hair,
and along the streets I go without food, quiet
bread does not sustain me, dawn driving me crazy
...I search for the liquid sound of your feet in the day.

I hunger for your little laugh,
and your hands the color of raging grain.
I hunger for the pale stones of your nails.
I want to eat you whole like an almond.

I want to eat the scalding rays of your beauty,
the haughty nose of your arrogant face;
I want to taste the fleeting shade of your lashes,

and I come hungry and I come smelling the twilight,
looking for you, for your hot heart,
like a wildcat in the solitary forest.

12

Full woman, fleshly apple, hot moon,
thick smell of seaweed, of mud and light crushed together,
what hidden light opens between your columns?
What ancient night does a man touch with his feelings?

Ah to love is to travel with water and with stars,
with suffocating winds and sudden storms of wheat dust.
To love is to fight with lightning,
our two bodies defeated by a single honey.

Kiss by kiss I travel your little infinities,
your borders, your rivers, your tiny villages;
and the heat of your genitals transformed by delight

runs through the tiny channels of my blood
until it explodes like a flower in the night;
until it is and is not—merely the flash of lightning in the darkness.

13

The light that rises from your feet to your hair,
the fullness that surrounds your delicate form—
this is not a pearl from the sea, nor is it cold silver.
You are bread, bread loved by fire.

The flour raised its barn for you,
and grew slowly during a fortunate age:
when grain doubled your breasts
my love was a coal in the ground.

Oh bread your forehead, your legs bread, bread your mouth,
bread that I devour and is born again with each morning's light,
belovéd colors of the bakeries:

fire gave you a lesson of blood,
flour taught you holiness,
and from bread you received your language and scent.

14

I don't have time to celebrate your hair.
One by one I count the strands and bless them.
Other lovers want to live in certainty,
I just want to be your stylist.

In Italy you were christened 'Medusa'
for the high curling light that came from your hair.
I call you my snare, my messy one:
My heart knows the door of your hair.

When you get lost in your own hair,
do not forget me, remember that I love you,
do not leave me wandering alone without your hair,

along the shadow world of all those roads
that have only darkness and fleeting pains,
until the sun rises again toward the tower of your hair.

15

For a long time the earth has known you:
you are compact, like bread or wood;
you are body, cluster of safe sustenance,
with the weight of acacia, the golden seed.

I know you exist not only because your eyes fly
and give birth to things, like an open window,
but because you were made and baked
in the city of sobs, in a speechless adobe oven.

The beings that pour out air or water or cold
or sloth, these are erased by the touch of time
as if they were dead before they crumbled.

You fall along with me like a stone in the tomb,
and so, just as our love cannot be consumed,
we will continue living along with this land.

16

I love the little piece of land that you are,
because in the meadow of planets
I have no other star. You tell
the vastness of the universe to me.

Your wide eyes are the light I receive
from defeated constellations.
Your skin throbs like those roads
that travel through a hail of meteors.

Your hips are the moon for me.
All of the sun is in your deep mouth and its delight,
so much burning light coming from your dark honey,

your heart scorched by long red rays.
And so I follow the fire of your kissing form,
small and planetary, my constellation and my country.

I do not love you as if you were a beach rose, or topaz
or an arrow of fiery carnations.
I love you as certain dark things are loved,
secretly, between the shadow and the soul.

I love you as the plant that does not bloom but carries
inside itself the light of those flowers,
and, thanks to your love, lives hidden in my body,
the dense fragrance that rises from the earth.

I love you without knowing how, or when, or where,
I love you straightforwardly without complexity or pride;
You see, I love you because I cannot love otherwise,

but in this way that neither you or I exist,
so close that your hand on my chest is mine,
so close that your eyes close when I fall asleep.

18

In the mountains you come as a breeze,
or a sudden stream of falling snow,
or as your own trembling hair, confirming
those ornaments of the sun high in the forest.

All the light from the Caucasus falls over your body
as the water in a small bowl endlessly
changes her clothes and her song,
transparent to each movement of the river.

In the mountains, over the roads of old armies
and below, furiously shining like a sword,
the waters move between walls of mineral hands.

Until suddenly you receive from the forest
the branch, or the lighting, of a few blue flowers
and the fresh arrow of a wild scent.

19

While the great foam of Isla Negra—
blue salt, sun in the waves—wets you,
I observe the work of the wasp
bent over the honey of his universe.

It comes and it goes in a faithful golden flight.
as if sliding along an invisible wire,
the elegance of his dance, the thirst of his waist,
and the murder of his malignant sting.

Oil and orange is your rainbow,
like an airplane in the grass,
with a hint of flying blades it disappears,

while you come out of the sea, naked,
and back into the world of salt and sun,
shimmering sculpture and sword of the sand.

My ugly one, you're a messy chestnut.
My beautiful one, you're lovely like the wind.
My ugly one, your mouth is big enough for two.
My beautiful one, your kisses are as fresh as watermelons.

My ugly one, where are they hiding your breasts?
They are as small as two cups of wheat.
I like to see those two moons of your chest,
gigantic badges of your sovereignty.

My ugly one, not even the sea has nails like yours for sale.
My beautiful one, flower by flower, star by star,
wave by wave, my love, I have counted your body.

My ugly one, I love you for your golden waist.
My beautiful one, I love you for the wrinkles of your forehead.
My love, I love you for your clarity and your darkness.

21

Oh that all your love might spread in my mouth,
not suffering a moment longer without spring.
My hands alone were sold to this pain.
Now, belovéd, come to me with your kisses.

Cover the month of light with your kisses,
close the door with your hair.
And as for me, don't forget that if I wake up and cry
it's because in my dreams I am only a lost child.

Looking through the leaves of your night-hands,
I find a touch of the wheat you meant for me,
a sparkling rapture of dark energy.

Oh belovéd, nothing but shadow
accompanies me in these dreams
and tells me the hour of the night.

How many times love, have I loved you without seeing you and
sometimes without memory,
without recognizing your look, without even looking, like a centaur
in dangerous places, in the burning afternoon:
there was only the smell of the wheat I love.

Maybe I saw you, suppose you were passing by lifting a glass,
in Angol, in the light of the summer moon,
or you were the body of that guitar
 I played in the darkness, the sound of a boundless sea.

I loved you without knowing it, and searched for your memory.
In the empty houses I went with a lantern to steal your portrait.
But I already knew what you were. Suddenly

I touched you, as you were alongside me, and it ended my life:
before my eyes you ruled me, and still you reign,
as a great fire in the forest, your kingdom of flame.

Light was fire, and bread was the rancorous moon,
and the jasmine told its starry secret,
and from that terrible love, pure soft hands
brought peace to my eyes and sun to my senses.

Oh love, how suddenly from these shameful wounds
you built an edifice of sweet resolve;
you defeated the perverse and jealous ones
and today we face the world as a single life.

So it is, and so it will be, until,
wild and sweet love, belovéd Matilde,
time will bring us the final flower of the day.

Without you, without me, without light we will not be.
Then beyond earth and shadow
the glow of our love will live on.

24

Love, love, clouds at the tower of heaven,
you rose as triumphant washerwomen,
and everything went up in blue, everything became a star:
the sea, the ship, the day were banished together.

Come see the cherry trees in the starry water
and the curving key of the swift universe,
come touch the instantaneous blue fire,
come before her petals are consumed.

There is nothing here but light, quantity, clusters,
open spaces for the virtues of the wind
to deliver the final secrets of the foam.

And among the celestial blue, submerged,
the powers of the air, the chambers of the sea.

25

Before I loved you, love, nothing was mine.
I wandered through the streets and the stores,
nothing mattered or had a name.
The world was like air, waiting.

I knew rooms full of ashes,
tunnels inhabited by the moon,
cruel hangars of goodbye,
questions that persisted in the sand.

Everything was empty, dead and silent,
fallen, abandoned and decayed.
Everything was inalienably strange.

Everything belonged to everyone and no one,
until your beauty and your poverty
filled the autumn with gifts.

Neither the color of the terrible dunes of Iquique,
nor the waters of Guatemala's Dulce river
can change your profile, forged in the wheat,
or the look of a large grape, or your singing mouth.

O heart of mine, out of the silences,
out of the mountains where vines reigned,
to the desolate plains of platinum,
in all pure places you are to be found.

But neither the sullen hands of stone mountains,
nor the snows of Tibet, nor the rocks of Poland—
nothing alters the form of your travelling fields;

thus clay or wheat, guitars or the grapes
of Chillan defend your territory,
imposing the mandate of this wild moon.

Naked, you are simple as one of your hands,
smooth, earthen, round, transparent,
you have the moon's lines, the apple trails.
Naked you are as naked as a naked sheaf of wheat.

Naked you are as blue as the night in Cuba,
with vines and stars in your hair.
Naked you are open and golden,
like summer in a church made of gold.

Naked you are as tiny as one of your fingernails,
curved, delicate, pink until morning comes,
and you go into the basement of the world,

that long tunnel of clothing and chores:
your clear light dims, gets dressed, drops its flowers,
and the world returns again into your naked hand.

Love, from grain to grain, planet to planet,
from the wind with its network of dark countries,
to the war with its bloody shoes,
or the horns of the day and the night.

Wherever we went, to islands or bridges or banners,
or to the fleeting violins of brittle Autumn,
happiness returned from our lips on the cup,
and pain stopped us with his lesson of tears.

In all Republics the wind unfolds
its guiltless flag, its freezing hair,
and then returns the flowers to their jobs.

But in us autumn never withered.
And in our country there sprouted and grew
a love with the rights of the morning dew.

29

You come from the poverty of southern houses,
the hard regions of cold and earthquakes,
where, even when the gods were rounded up and executed,
they still gave us life-lessons in the dirt.

You are a little clay horse, a kiss
of black earth, a clay poppy,
dove of twilight that flew along our roads,
penny bank that holds the tears of our children.

Girl, you've kept your poor heart,
your feet accustomed to the rocks,
your mouth that did not always eat bread or delight.

You are the poor south, where my soul came from:
in heaven your mother is washing clothes
with my mother. This is why I chose you, my companion.

You have the needles of the island pine,
its flesh worked by centuries of time,
veins that knew sea timbers,
green blood fallen from heaven to memory.

Nobody had picked up my lost heart,
between so many roots, in the bitter cold
of the sun multiplied by the fury of water,
there lives the shadow that travels with me.

So you left the south, like an island
populated and crowned with feathers and wood
and I smelled the scent of a wandering forest.

I found the dark honey that I knew in the forest,
and I played on your hips and your shaded petals
that were born with me and built my soul.

With southern laurels and the spices of Lota,
I crown you king of my bones,
and you cannot refuse that crown
that put balsam and leaves on this earth.

You are, like that lover, from the green provinces:
from there we pulled the clay that runs in our blood.
In the city we walked, like so many, lost
and worried that the market had closed.

Belovéd, your shadow smells of plums,
your eyes hidden in the Southern roots,
your heart a penny-bank made of birds.

Your heart is as smooth as stones in the river,
your kisses like a rain of grapes,
and beside you I live with the earth.

32

At morning the house rebels with the truth
of linens and feathers, the start of the day,
directionless, wandering like a poor little boat
between the horizons of order and sleep.

Things want to drag traces,
adhesions without reason, cold legacies,
the papers that hide wrinkled voices,
and in the bottle, wine that wants yesterday to continue.

Cleaning, you shimmer like a bee,
touching the lost regions of darkness,
conquering light with your brilliant energy,

And then you built a new clarity:
things obey the wind of life,
and order establishes its bread and its dove.

Afternoon

33

Now we're going home, my love,
where the vine climbs the steps.
Before you even reach your bedroom there will have come
the naked summer of your honeysuckle feet.

Our wandering kisses traveled the world:
Armenia, that thick drop of unearthed honey,
Ceylon, green dove, and the Yangtze river separating
with ancient patience the day from the night.

And now my love, by the breaking sea,
we fly into the wall like two blind birds,
into the nest of a distant spring.

Because love cannot move without stopping,
the wall, or sea-stones, are our lives:
to their own countries our kisses return.

You are the daughter of the sea and the cousin of spice.
As swimmer, your body is pure water.
As cook, your blood is living earth,
and your customs are flowers and land.

Your eyes go to the water and raise the waves,
your hands go to the earth and break the seeds,
the water and soil have deep properties
that in you join together like the religion of clay.

Nymph, your body cut the turquoise
and resurrected flowers in the kitchen,
thereby you assume all that exists,

and finally you sleep surrounded by my arms, away
from the grim darkness, so that you can rest,
vegetables, seaweed, herbs: this is the lather of your dreams.

Your hand went flying up to my eyes,
light opened like a rose,
sand and sky throbbed like
the last beehive cut into turquoises.

Your hand touched syllables that tinkled, cups,
flasks filled with yellow oils,
blossoms, waterfalls, and above all, love,
love itself: your pure hand preserved the spoons.

The evening came. The night crept stealthily
around the dream of a man in his celestial capsule.
A sad wild smell escaped from the honeysuckle.

And your hand, back from its flight, having flown
to shut the wings I thought I'd lost,
passes over my eyes and is devoured by the shadows.

My heart, queen of celery and bowl,
little leopard made of thread and onion,
I like to see your tiny empire,
weapons of wax, wine, and oil,

of garlic, of land opened by your hands,
the blue stuff burning in your hands,
of the transformation of dreams into food,
of the snake coiled in the hose.

You with your mower raising the perfume,
you with the way of soap in the foam,
you, climbing my crazy ladders and stairs,

you, managing the symptoms of my writing,
and find in the sand of my notebook,
the letters that seek your missing mouth.

Oh love, oh crazy lightning and threat of violet,
you climb with your new ladder
the castle that time had crowned with haze,
the pale walls of my closed heart.

No one will know it was tenderness
that built crystals as hard as cities,
and that blood opened lonely tunnels
which, without your sovereignty, might depose even winter.

For this, love, your mouth, your hair, your light, your sorrows,
were the ancestors of life, the sacred
gifts of the rain, of nature,

that receive and lift the weight of the grain,
the secret storm of wine in the cellars,
the flash of wheat on the floor.

Your house sounds like a train in the afternoon,
humming of bees, songs of pans,
cascading lists made by the rain;
your laughter develops its palm tree song.

The light blue wall converses with the stone,
comes as a boy with a singing telegram,
and between the green voice of two figs
Homer walks with his quiet shoes.

Only here the city has no voice, crying.
Here is not eternity, not sonatas, not lips or horns
but a speech full of waterfalls and lions,

and you climb, sing, run, walk, fall,
plant, sew, cook, nail, write, return.
Or you depart, and know that the winter begins.

But I forget your hands have satisfied
the roots, watering tangled roses
until your fingerprints flourished
in the fullness of nature.

The hoe and the water are your animals,
they accompany you, biting and licking the earth,
and thus you go, working, releasing
fertility, fresh fire of carnations.

Bees ask for the love and honor of your hands,
that in the confused earth have their transparent lineage,
and even in my heart have opened agriculture,

so I'm like burnt stone
that sings suddenly along with you
because it has received the forest water you brought to me.

40

Green was the silence, wet was the light,
June was shaking like a butterfly,
and in the southern domain, from the sea and the rocks,
came Matilde, traveler of noon.

You were full of iron flowers,
seaweed that the south wind torments and forgets,
still white, even cracked by the devouring sand
your hands picked the spikes of the sand.

I love your pure gifts, your skin of unbreached stone,
your nails offering the joy of the sun,
your mouth brimming with every ecstasy,

but here in my house beside the abyss,
give me the torture of silence,
the sea's forgotten pavilion in the sand.

Misery of January, when the indifferent
noon establishes its equation in the sky,
a solid gold like the wineglass filled with wine
fills the earth to its blue limits.

Misery of time like grapes,
small pools of bitter green,
confused, secret tears of the day
until storms reveal their sweetness.

Yes, germs and pain, every throbbing,
terrified thing, until the breaking light of January,
ripens and ferments, as fruits are fermented.

Sorrows will lessen, the soul
will be given some wind, and the house
will be clean with fresh bread on the table.

Bright days balanced by seawater,
concentrated like the insides of a yellow stone
whose honey splendors do not destroy disorder:
rectangular purity is preserved.

Crackling, yes, time like fire or bees
and the green task of diving into leaves,
until towards the tops of the foliage
a sparkling world fades out and whispers.

Be that fire, burning the summer crowds,
the fire that builds an Eden with a few leaves
because the dark-faced land does not want suffering,

but freshness or fire, water or bread for everyone,
and that nothing should divide men
but the evening sun or the moon or the flowers.

43

Now we're going home, my love,
where the vine climbs the steps.
Before you even reach your bedroom there will have come
the naked summer of your honeysuckle feet.

Our wandering kisses traveled the world:
Armenia, that thick drop of unearthed honey,
Ceylon, green dove, and the Yangtze river separating
with ancient patience the day from the night.

And now my love, by the breaking sea,
we fly into the wall like two blind birds,
into the nest of a distant spring.

Because love cannot move without stopping,
the wall, or sea-stones, are our lives:
to their own countries our kisses return.

44

You will know that I do not love you and that I love you
since of two modes is this life composed:
the spoken word has its wing of silence,
fire its cold half.

I love you so that I can begin to love you
so I can begin again to love you to infinity,
and never stop loving you,
thus I do not love you yet.

I love you and I do not love you, as if I held
in my hands the keys to happiness
and an uncertain, unhappy fate.

My love has two lives to arm itself.
And so when I love you I love you not,
and when I love you, I do love you.

45

Don't go far from me, not for one single day, because,
because...I don't know how to say it, the day is long
and I will be waiting, as in railway stations
when some of the trains fall asleep.

Don't leave me for even an hour for then
the drops of insomnia will join together
and perhaps all the smoke that roams, looking for a home
will come and kill my lost heart.

Oh let not your silhouette be broken in the sand,
oh let not your eyelids be demolished with the absence:
do not leave me for even a moment, belovéd,

for in that moment you've gone so far
I will cross all the earth asking
if you will return or if you will leave me dying.

Of all the stars I have admired, wet
by various rivers and rains,
I chose only the one I loved,
and since then I sleep with the night.

Wave after wave after wave,
sea-green, cold green, green branch,
yet I chose only a single wave:
the indivisible wave of your body.

All raindrops, all roots,
all the threads of light came,
came to see me sooner or later.

I wanted your hair.
And yet from all the gifts of my country
I chose only your savage heart.

47

Behind me, on a branch, I want to see you.
Little by little you become fruit.
It cost you nothing to rise from these roots,
singing in a syllable of sap.

Here you'll be the first fragrant flower
in the temple of a converted kiss,
until sun and earth, blood and sky
grant you delight and sweetness.

In the branch you see your hair,
your image ripens in the trees
bringing the leaves closer to my thirst,

and your substance fills my mouth
with the kiss that rose from the earth,
with your blood the belovéd fruit.

48

Two happy lovers make one bread,
a single drop of moonlight on the grass,
their two shadows walk together as one,
leaving a single empty sun in the bed.

From all truths they chose the day,
for it was not bound with ropes but with a scent,
and they violated neither the spirit nor the letter of that law.
Happiness is a transparent tower.

Air and wine accompanies those lovers,
the night delights them with its joyous petals:
they have the right to every carnation.

Two happy lovers have no end or death,
they are born and they die many times while living,
they live as nature: eternally.

It's today. Yesterday everything was falling
between fingers of light and sleepy eyes
tomorrow will come with green steps.
Nobody stops the river of dawn.

Nobody stops the river of your hands,
your sleepy eyes, belovéd,
you are the trembling of time that passes
between high noon and the sun's shadow.

And the sky that closes over your wings
taking you and bringing you to my arms
was timely, a mysterious courtesy.

So I sing to the day and the moon,
to the sea, to time ,to all the planets,
to your voice by day, and to your body by night.

50

Cotapos says your laughter falls
like a hawk from a sharp tower,
and indeed you travel the garden of the world
with a single flash from your starry family.

Falling, and tiny, you leap the tongues of rain,
the diamond waters, the light full of bees,
and there where previously only bearded silence had lived,
you explode into a sun and stars;

the sky collapses with the grim night,
flowers and bells burn in the full moon,
and horses are saddled by their riders.

Because you are as tiny as you are,
let laughter fall from your little meteor,
powering the name of nature.

51

Your laughter belongs to a tree split
by lightning, by the silver lightning
that falls from the shattered glass of the sky
and cuts a tree into two with one sword.

Only in the snowy highlands
is a laugh like yours born, my darling
it is the laughter of air rising through the heights,
my belovéd, it is the tao of evergreens.

My Andean woman, my naked Chilean
you are cut open by knives of dark laughter:
the night, and the morning, and the honey of afternoon—

so that birds may leap to heaven from the bushes,
when, just like that killing light,
your laughter rips open the tree of life.

You sing to sun and sky with your song.
Your voice threshes the wheat of the day.
The pines speak with their green tongue.
All the birds of winter sing.

The steps of the sea's cellar
are filled with bells, chains, and groans,
clinking metal and utensils,
sounds like the wheels of a caravan.

But it is only your voice I hear, rising
with the speed and precision of an arrow,
lowering with the gravity of rain,

Your voice scatters the highest swords,
becomes laden with violets,
and goes with me as I cross the sky.

53

Here is the bread, the wine, the table, the dwelling,
the necessities of man, of woman, of life.
An ecstatic peace ran to this place.
By this light the common fire burned.

Hail to your two hands as they move, preparing
the simple creations of singing and kitchen.
Hail to the integrity of your beating hands,
blessings on the ballerina dancing with the broom.

Those rough rivers with their waters and threats,
that tormented tent of foam,
those burning reefs and shallows,

are now the calm of your blood in mine.
This starry blue channel of night
is the endless simplicity of tenderness.

Evening

54

Splendid reason, transparent demon
of absolute fruits, of the respectable noon,
here we are at last, alone yet not lonely,
far from the city's madness.

When the pure snare surrounds its dove
and fire honors the peace with its food,
you and I shall praise this heavenly creation!
Reason and love live naked in this house together.

Furious sleep, river of bitter certainty,
decisions harder than the dreams of a hammer
fell into the lovers' double cup.

Until they rise in the balance as twins,
reason and love are as two wings.
This is how clarity was constructed.

55

Thorns, broken glass, diseases, and crying
besiege the happy honey of day and night,
and these do not serve the tower, nor the journey, nor the walls.
Happiness passes across the peace of sleepers.

Pain rises and lowers and surrounds your shovels,
and no man is without this movement,
no birth, no shelter, no enclosure.
One must consider these things.

In love, closed eyes are worthless,
deep layers away from the stinking wounded,
or that which step by step captures the flag.

Because life hits us like rage, like a river,
and opens a bloody tunnel through which we watch
an immense family of pain.

Get used to seeing a shadow behind me,
and your hands, out of spite, clear
as the creations of the sea at morning.

Envy suffers and dies, exhausted by my singing,
one by one its sad captains are dying.
I say "love" and the world is filled with birds.
Every syllable of mine brings in spring.

Then you, my flower-girl, my heart, my belovéd
you are before my eyes like the gardens of heaven;
I look again and see you lying on the ground.

I have seen the sun change grapes into a face.
Looking up at the sky, belovéd, I recognize your steps.
Matilde, my belovéd, my crown: welcome home.

57

Those liars who said I'd lost the moon,
who prophesied a future of sand,
and gossiped so much with cold tongues—
they tried to ban the flower of the universe.

"He sings no more the rising amber
of sirens, he is left with only people,"
said those who chew their papers incessantly,
patronizing my oblivious guitar.

I threw flaming spears into their eyes,
daggers that came from the love which pierced your heart and mine.
I reclaimed the jasmine left behind in your footprints.

I got lost at night without the light of your eyelids,
and when light surrounded me
I was born again, the owner of my own ignorance.

58

Between the iron swords of literature
I pass like a lost sailor,
through unfamiliar corners and singing,
because…because if I don't, then there's nothing left.

From the tortured islands I brought
my storming music, my gusts of crazy rain,
and I grew accustomed to the languor of natural things,
they guided my wild heart.

Thus when the teeth of literature
tried to bite my honest heels,
I went without noticing, singing along with the wind,

to the rainy storehouses of my childhood,
to cold forests of the remote South,
to wherever my life is filled with your scent.

59
(for G. M.)

Poor poets, whom life and death pursued
with the same grim tenacity,
they are covered now with unfeeling ceremony,
they are delivered now into the ritual of the funeral's mouth.

They—dark as pebbles—now
lying behind the arrogant horses,
governed finally by intruders,
among ushers, sleep without silence.

Before we were even certain that the dead had died
the funeral had been turned into a wretched feast,
with turkeys, pigs, and other orators.

Some had watched him die, and then insulted his death
only because his mouth is shut
and cannot contest their song.

60

It hurt you that there were those who wanted to hurt me,
and the pain of the venom directed at me
is filtered between my work
and you, leaving only a stain made of rust and insomnia.

I do not want to see hatred lurking, my love,
in the florid moon of your forehead.
I do not want see in your dreams the hatred of others,
that neglected crown of knives.

Wherever I walk, bitter footsteps follow.
Where I laugh, horrible grimaces mock me.
Where I sing, jealousy curses me, laughing and biting.

And it is that, love, that shadow which life has given me:
an empty suit limps after me,
like a scarecrow made from bloody smiles.

Love brought along his tail of pain,
with its spines like frozen lightning,
and we closed our eyes so that nothing,
no wound could separate us.

This crying is not the fault of your eyes:
your hands did not thrust this sword,
your feet did not seek this way.
Your heart was made from dark honey.

When love came like a tremendous wave,
we were smashed against a hard stone;
we kneaded a single flour,

and pain fell upon another sweet face,
thus the light of an open season
was consecrated as spring's wound.

Woe is me, woe is us, belovéd.
All we wanted was love, love,
and among the many modes of sorrow
it was left us to be wounded so.

We wanted you and I to be us,
the you of your kiss, the I of bread made in secret,
and that was all, eternally simple,
until hatred came through the window.

They hate us, who did not love our love,
or any love; the dispossessed,
like a lost lounge chair,

until it is reduced to ash,
the menacing face it had worn,
itself fading with the twilight.

63

Not only did I walk the deserts, where rocksalt
is the only pink rose, the flower of a buried sea,
but by the banks of rivers that cut through the snow.
The bitter heights of the mountains know my steps.

Tangled, whistling region of my wild country,
mortal kiss of vines, those chains of the forest,
wet lament of flocks of birds, releasing their chill cries:
oh lost land of pain and tears.

Not only are these mine—poisonous copper skin
and salt laid out like sleeping statues covered with snow—
but also the vineyard and the cherry tree, rewarded by spring.

These are mine, and I belong as a black atom
to the dry lands and the light of autumn in the grapes,
to the metallic country of high, snowy towers.

From so much love, my life had become violet colored,
and I was heading like a blind bird
toward your window, love,
and you heard the sound of a broken heart.

There I stood in the darkness of your chest,
being nothing and knowing nothing, I went to the tower of wheat,
I rose to live between your hands.
I rose from the sea to your joy.

Nobody can say what I owe you, my love; it's clear
I do owe you, belovéd; like the roots of the evergreen,
I am in your debt.

All I owe you is as the stars;
what I owe you is like a well in the wilderness
where roaming bolts of lightning keep the time.

65

Matilde, where are you? I noticed down
between my tie and my heart
a certain melancholy in my chest.
You were suddenly absent.

I needed the light of your energy,
and looked around devouring hope,
I looked at the void which has no home,
only tragic windows.

The roof listens in its pure silence
to the leafless old rain falling,
feathers which the night had imprisoned:

this is how I wait for you—like a lonely house,
waiting for you to return and live in me,
otherwise, these windows, they will hurt me.

I don't love you except because I love you,
and from loving you and not loving you I go,
and from waiting for you when I am not waiting for you
my heart moves from ice to fire.

I love you because I love you,
I hate you endlessly, and by hating I am praying to you.
The measure of my changing love
was that, not seeing you, I loved blindly.

Maybe the light of January will consume,
with its cruel rays, my whole heart,
robbing me of the keys to eternal calm.

In this story I die,
and I will die because of my desire,
because I love you, love, because I love your blood and your fire.

The great Southern rain falls on Isla Negra
as a single transparent and heavy drop,
the sea opens its cold leaves and receives it,
and earth learns the wet destiny of a glass.

My soul, give me in your kisses the salt
water of those seas, the honey of the land,
the wet fragrance of a thousand heavenly lips,
the sacred patience of the sea in winter.

Something calls us, all doors open by themselves,
the water relates its abundant rumors to the windows,
the sky grows down, until it touches the grass.

It weaves and unweaves its celestial network
with time, salt, whispers, growing, roads,
a woman, a man, and winter in the ground.

The girl of the woods did not come walking:
suddenly she was there sitting on the bricks,
old flowers of the sea covered her head;
her gaze held roots of sadness.

There she sat staring at our empty lives,
the going and being and traveling and returning on the earth,
the day shedding its gentle petals.
The girl of the woods watched without seeing.

The girl crowned by the ancient waters,
she watched us there with her defeated eyes.
Know that we live in a remote network

of time and water and waves and sound and rain,
not knowing if we exist or if we are just part of her dream.
This is the story of the girl of the woods.

Perhaps 'not to be' is to be without your presence,
to be without you cutting the afternoon
like a blue flower, without you walking
later by the fog and the bricks,

without the light you carry in your hand,
which perhaps others don't see as golden,
which perhaps no one even knew was growing
like the first red of the rose,

without your being—anyway, without you coming,
sharp, provocative, to know my life,
a gust from the rosebushes, wheat from the wind,

and since then I am because you are,
and since then you are, I am, we are,
for love I will be, you will be, we will be.

Perhaps though I am hurt I will not go bloodied
by the lightning of your life,
halfway into the forest the water stops me,
the rain that falls along with the sky.

Then I touched the rain-soaked heart:
there I know that your eyes penetrated
to the vast country of my grief
as a solitary whisper of shadow emerges:

Who's there? Who's there? But it has no name,
leaf or dark water that beats
the depths of the forest to deafness along the way;

and so my love, I knew that I was wounded
and no one spoke there except the shadow,
the wandering night, the kiss of the rain.

From sorrow to sorrow love crosses its islands
and plants its roots after being watered with tears,
and nobody can, nobody can evade the steps
of the heart that run silent and carnivorous.

So you and I are looking for a hole, another planet,
where the salt doesn't touch your hair,
where pains do not grow because of me
where bread rises without agony.

A planet tangled in distance and leaves,
a wasteland, a stone, cruel and uninhabited,
with our hands we wanted to make this hard nest,

without damage or wound or word,
but our love was not like that. It was a crazy city,
where people turned pale on balconies.

My love, the winter returns to its barracks.
The ground puts out its yellow gifts,
and we pass our hand over a distant country,
over the hair of its geography.

We leave! Today! Roll on wheels, ships, church bells,
aircraft hardened by the infinite day,
toward the smell of the island's bridal suite,
the ground –grain of our horizontal bliss.

Come on! Let's go! Grab your crown and rise
and fall and run and sing with the air and with me
as we go on the trains of Arabia or Tocopilla,

just a little trip to distant pollen,
the piercing poverty of rags and gardenias,
ruled by the shoeless monarchs of poverty.

73

Perhaps you will recall that brusque man
who came out of the darkness like a knife,
and how before we knew, he knew:
he saw the smoke and decided it was coming from fire.

The pale woman with black hair
emerged like a fish out of the deep,
and between the two of them they built an anti-love
machine gun loaded with numerous teeth.

Man and woman leveled mountains and gardens,
went down to the rivers, scaled the walls,
and raised at the heights their terrible artillery.

That's when love knew it was love.
And when I raised my eyes to your name
your heart suddenly decided my path.

74

The road wet by the waters of August
shines like a slice of the full moon,
in the fat clarity of an apple,
in the middle of autumn's fruit.

Fog, space or sky, the vague net of day
fills with cold dreams, sounds, and fish,
the mist of the islands fights with the land,
and the sea beats over the light of Chile.

Everything is concentrated, like the metal
hidden in leaves. The winter denies its ancestry
and only the blind are left, ceaseless and solitary,

subject only to the silent riverbed
of movement, goodbye of the journey, the path:
goodbye. The tears of nature are falling.

This is the house, the sea, and the flag.
We wandered by other long walls.
We could obtain neither the sound nor the door
in the absence, which was as if from the dead.

And finally the house opened its silence,
and we went in to walk upon the abandonment,
the dead rats, the hollow goodbye,
the water that cried in the pipes.

She cried, she cried, this house cried day and night,
she moaned with the spiders, broken open,
she whipped herself with her black eyes,

and suddenly we return her to life,
we populate her and she does not recognize us:
you have to flourish and not remember.

Diego Rivera, with the patience of a bear,
sought the emerald of the forest in his painting,
or vermillion, that sudden flower of blood:
it reflected the light of the world in your portrait.

He painted the imperious mask of your nose,
the sparkle of your wild eyes,
your nails that feed the envy of the moon,
your summer skin, your foolish mouth.

He gave you two heads of volcanos lit
by fire, by love, by native blood,
and over those two golden faces of clay

you are covered in the helmet of courageous burning,
and there secretly remain entangled
my eyes in the full tower: your hair.

Today is today with the weight of all time gone,
with the wings of all that will be tomorrow,
today is the South Sea, the old age of water,
and the composition of a new day.

In your mouth, open to the moonlight
appeared the petals of an emaciated day,
and yesterday came trotting by this shady street,
to remind us that he is dead.

Today, yesterday, and tomorrow are eaten as they pass,
we consume days like a burning calf,
our cattle waiting also with their days numbered,

but in your heart time cast its flour,
while my love built a mud oven in Temuco:
you are the daily bread of my soul.

I don't have never. I don't have always. In the sand
victory left his doomed footprints.
I am a poor man who is willing to love his fellow men.
I don't know who you are. No, I don't sell thorns.

Someone will perhaps know that I wove no bloody
crowns, that I fought the mockery,
and that in truth I filled the high tide of my soul.
I repaid meanness with doves.

I have no never because I was…
I am…different, I always will be. And in the name
of my changing love I proclaim purity.

Death is only a stone of oblivion.
I love you; I kiss joy in your mouth.
Bring firewood. We'll make a fire on the mountain.

Night

At night, belovéd, tie your heart to mine
and in that dream we will defeat the darkness
like twin drums beating in the wild
against the heavy wall of wet leaves.

Night crossing: black ember of sleep
intercepts the thread of earthly orbs
as punctual as a headlong train,
the cold stone and its shadow dragged forever.

For that, love, tie up the pure movement,
the tenacity that beats in your chest
with the wings of a submerged swan,

for all the questions of a starry sky
our dream responds with a single key,
with a single closed door in the dark.

From travel and pains I return, my love,
to your voice, to your hand flying on the guitar,
to the fire that interrupted fall with its kisses,
to the movement of night in the heavens.

For all men I ask bread and a kingdom.
I ask for land for the farmer with no future.
Nobody should expect surrender from my blood or my singing,
but I cannot resign from your love without dying.

So play the waltz of the silent moon
the little folk song of water in the guitar
until my broken head lies dreaming:

all the labors of my life wove
this canopy where your hand lives and flies,
guarding the night of this sleepy traveler.

You are mine. Rest with your dream in my dream.
Love, pain, work... all must sleep now.
Turn the night on its invisible wheels,
and near to me you are as pure as sleeping amber.

No one else, love, will sleep with my dreams
You will—go we will go—together, through the waters of time.
No one will travel through the shadows with me,
only you, forever young, forever sun, forever moon.

You already opened your delicate fists
and let those soft signs fall aimlessly,
your eyes closed like two gray wings,

while I follow the water that you carry, the water that carries me:
the night, the world, the wind divines its destination,
and I am no longer with you, but only your dream.

My love, at the closing of this night door,
I ask for a journey through that dark enclosure:
close your dreams, enter into the heaven in my eyes,
spread yourself in my blood like a wide river.

Goodbye, goodbye cruel clarity
falling into the bag of all past days,
goodbye to every misfortune of clock or orange,
and here's to you oh shadow, intermittent companion!

In this ship or water or death or new life,
once again we are united, we sleep, we rise,
we are the marriage of night and blood.

I do not know who lives or dies or rests or wakes,
only that it is your heart which delivers
in my chest the gifts of the dawn.

It is good, my love, to feel you near me in the night,
invisible in your sleep, solemnly nocturnal,
while I untangle my worries
as if they were tangled nets.

Absent, your heart dreams by flying,
but your abandoned body breathes and seeks me
without finding me, thus completing my dream
as a flower is doubled by its shadow.

Rising up tomorrow, you will be one of those who live,
but the borders we lost in the night,
that being and not-being where we found ourselves

some of those come close to the light of life,
and they are marked with a seal from that darkness
which has branded its secret creatures with fire.

Once again, love, the network of day destroys
jobs, wheels, fires, gasps, goodbyes,
and in the night we bring swaying wheat
that noon obtained from light and earth.

Only the moon in the middle of his pure book
sustains the columns of the river of heaven.
Our bedroom adopts the patience of gold,
while your hands go and go, preparing the night.

Oh love, oh night, oh dome enclosed by a river
of impenetrable waters in the shadow of heaven,
showing and drowning its storm-washed grapes,

until we have only this single dark place,
a cup in which star dust is falling,
a drop in the pulse of a long, slow river.

85

From the sea to the streets runs the hazy fog
like the breath of an ox buried in the cold,
and long tongues of water accumulate over us
covering the month that had promised us heaven.

Come fall, swishing honeycomb of leaves,
when your banner beats on the people
crazy women sing farewell to the rivers
and horses sigh at Patagonia.

There is a vine in your face at evening,
which grows in the silent love carried
until those horses thunder out of heaven.

I lean on the fire of your body overnight,
and it is not only your breasts I love but the autumn
that also to this fog gives up its foreign blood.

O Southern Cross, O triple-leaf of fragrant phosphorus,
today, with four sweet kisses, beauty penetrated you
and passed on through my shade and my shadow:
the moon went on revolving in the cold.

Then with my love, my belovéd—o diamonds
of blue frost, serenity of heaven,
returned light—you appeared to me and filled the night
with your four trembling wine cellars.

O beating fish of silver, polished and pure,
green cross, sprig of glowing shadow,
firefly to the symmetry of heaven condemned,

rest in me, close your eyes and mine.
For just a moment sleep with the night of men:
your four starry numbers burn in me.

Three sea birds, three rays of light, three scissors,
cruised through the cold sky toward Antofagasta,
their motion making the air tremble,
making everything tremble like a wounded flag.

Solitude, give me the sign of your incessant origin,
the lonely road of cruel birds,
the beating that without doubt comes before
honey, music, the sea, birth.

(It is only sustained by a timeless face
like a solemn flower that goes on endlessly
to cover the sheer multitude of heaven.)

Cold flying wings of ocean, of Archipelago,
you were flying toward the sands of Northern Chile.
And night closed its starry latch.

88

The month of March is back with its hidden light:
huge fish glide through heaven,
the strange silent breath of earth moves,
and one by one, things fall silent.

Fortunately in this crisis of climate change,
you reunited the lives of the sea with those of the fire:
gray movement of the ship of winter,
the shape that love gave to the guitar.

O love, rose wet by mermaids and sea-foam,
fire that dances and climbs the invisible staircase,
and wakes in the bloody tunnel of insomnia,

to be consumed by those waves in the sky.
The sea forgets its blessings and its lions,
and the world itself falls down into a dark prison.

When I die I want your hands on my eyes.
I want the light and the wheat of your belovéd hands
once more to pass their newness over me:
to feel the gentleness that changed my destiny.

I want you to live while I sleep; while I wait for you
I want your ears still to hear the wind,
for you still to smell the sea that we so loved together,
for your feet to walk the beach that was once beneath us.

I want what I loved to go on living,
you whom I loved and sang above all things,
for this you must go on blooming, little flower-girl,

so that all my love has arranged for you may come to pass,
so that your hair may fall across my shadow,
so that you may know the reason for these songs.

I thought I was dying. I felt the cold close in,
and how I had lived only to lose you:
your mouth was the land of my days and nights,
and your body the Republic founded by my kisses.

At that moment all my books ended, along with
friendship, the treasures I had relentlessly accumulated,
the transparent house that you and I built.
Everything ceased to exist except your eyes.

Because love, while life harasses us,
is simply a wave higher than all the other waves,
but oh when death comes to touch your door,

there is only your gaze toward the void,
only your clarity for non-existence,
only your love left to close the shade.

91

Age covers us over like the rain.
Endless and barren is this time.
A salt plume touches your face,
a leak gnaws at my suit.

Time does not distinguish between my hands
and the flight of oranges in your hands:
it picks at your life with snow and axe:
your life is my life.

This life of mine that I gave to you
is full of years, like a tree full of fruit.
Grapes return to the earth.

And even down there is time,
waiting, raining down over the dust,
eager to wash away even the absence.

My love if I should die and you do not,
give sorrow no more territory.
My love if you should die and I do not,
there will be no universe like the one where we lived.

Dust on the wheat, sand on the beach,
time, the wandering water, the vagrant wind,
all blew us away like grain in the water.
We could not find ourselves in such a time.

To that meadow in which we found ourselves—
oh little infinity—we return.
But this love, love, has no end.

And just as it had no birth,
it has no death, it is like a long river,
changing only the earth and her lips.

If some day your chest should stop moving,
if something stops burning through your veins,
if the voice in your mouth has no more words,
if your hands forget to fly and fall asleep,

Matilde, love, leave your lips parted
because that final kiss must last with me,
must stand still forever in your mouth,
so that it may accompany me in my death.

I will die kissing your cold crazy mouth
embracing the lost fruits of your body,
and seeking the light from your closed eyes.

And so when the earth receives our embrace
we shall lose ourselves in a single death,
to live forever in the eternity of a kiss.

If I die, survive me with such pure force
that you wake the fury of all that is pale and cold,
from south to south raise your indelible eyes
from sunrise to sunset let your guitar's mouth ring.

I don't want your laughter or your steps to waver.
I don't want my legacy of laughter to die.
Don't bother checking for a pulse. I'm gone.
Live in my absence as if it were a house.

Such a large house is absence
that you pass right through her walls
and must hang pictures in the air.

Such a vivid house is absence
that though I am dead, I watch you live,
and if you should suffer then I will die again.

95

Whoever loved as we do? Find
the ancient ashes of a heart that burned
and there let fall one by one our kisses
until that abandoned flower is revived.

Love the love that consumed this fruit
and descended to the earth with courage and power:
you and I are the light that continues on,
the delicate, unswerving seed.

The love that was buried for cold weather,
for snow and spring, for neglect and autumn—
come closer to the light of a new apple,

the freshness opens another wound,
like the old love, walking in silence
past an eternity of buried mouths.

I think to myself—this time in which you loved me
will be replaced by another blue,
there will be another skin over these bones,
other eyes will see the spring.

None of those who tried to tie down time,
those who conversed with smoke—
governments, smugglers, passers-by—
none of them will continue moving in those ropes.

They will pass away, those cruel gods wearing glasses,
the hairy meat-eaters with their book,
the ladybugs and the little birds.

And when the world is freshly washed
other eyes appear in the water
and wheat grows without tears.

You must fly this time. But where?
No wings, no airplane, and no doubt. You must fly.
You've already passed the point of no return
and so far you've not lifted the passenger's feet.

You must fly in every moment like
eagles, like insects, like the days;
you must overpower the rings of Saturn
and establish new bells there.

Already not enough shoes or roads,
already the earth is not good for wanderers,
already roots have crossed the night,

and you appear in another star,
resolved to impermanence,
changed, at last, into a poppy.

98

And this word, this paper written
for thousands of hands by a single hand,
this is not for you; it is not good for your dreams,
it falls to the ground and there it remains.

No matter that light or praise
are spilled in and out of the cup,
unless you are the persistent trembling of the wine,
unless it was your mouth that took the stain of Amaranth.

The word wants no more that tardy syllable
that builds and re-builds the coral reef
of my memories, the burning smoke.

It wants nothing more than to write your name,
and although my gloomy love is silent for now,
later he will tell it to the spring.

Other days will arrive, the silence
of plants and planets will be understood.
Many noble things will happen.
Violins will smell of the moon.

Perhaps bread will be as you are,
your voice, your wheat,
other things will speak with your voice:
the lost horses of Autumn.

Although it won't be arranged as it is now,
love will fill huge barrels,
like the ancient honey of shepherds,

and you in the dust of my heart
(where there stand immense storehouses),
you will come and go between the watermelons.

100

In the midst of the earth I clear away
emeralds so I can see you,
and you will be there drawing spikes of grain
with a water pen full of messages.

What a world! What profound decorations!
What ship sailing the sweetness!
And you and I may be a jewel as well!
There will be no more division among bells,

there will be nothing but the open air,
apples carried by the wind,
the succulent book of the orchard.

And in that place where carnations breathe
we will create a sort of clothes
that can resist eternity's victorious kiss.